1. CREWNECK CARDIGAN

Size:	Small	Medium	Large	Ex-Large
Chest Measurement:	32-34"	36-38"	40-42"	44-46"
Finished Chest Measurement:	35½"	39½"	43½"	47½"

Size Note: Instructions are written for size Small with sizes Medium, Large, and Ex-Large in braces { }. Instructions will be easier to read if you circle all the numbers pertaining to your size. If only one number is given, it applies to all sizes.

MATERIALS
Bedspread Weight Cotton Thread (size 10):
   2,185{2,455-2,675-2,915} yards
Steel crochet hook, size 8 (1.50 mm) **or** size needed
   for gauge
Tapestry needle
⅜" Buttons - 6
Sewing needle and thread

GAUGE: In pattern, 6 Shells = 3"; 16 rows = 3¾"

Gauge Swatch: 3"w x 3¾"h
Ch 39.
Work same as Body for 16 rows.
Finish off.

Cardigan is worked in one piece to armhole.

STITCH GUIDE

SHELL
(2 Dc, ch 2, 2 dc) in ch-4 sp indicated.

DECREASE (uses next ch-1 sp and next st)
YO, insert hook in next ch-1 sp, YO and pull up a loop, YO and draw through 2 loops on hook, YO, insert hook in next st, YO and pull up a loop, YO and draw through 2 loops on hook, YO and draw through all 3 loops on hook (**counts as one dc**).

BODY
Ch 417{465-513-561}.

Row 1: Sc in second ch from hook and in next ch, ★ ch 4, skip next 4 chs, sc in next 2 chs; repeat from ★ across: 69{77-85-93} ch-4 sps.

Row 2 (Right side): Ch 3 (**counts as first dc, now and throughout**), turn; work Shell in each ch-4 sp across, skip next sc, dc in last sc: 69{77-85-93} Shells.

Note: Loop a short piece of thread around any stitch to mark Row 2 as **right** side.

Row 3: Ch 5 (**counts as first dc plus ch 2, now and throughout**), turn; 2 sc in next Shell (ch-2 sp), (ch 4, 2 sc in next Shell) across, ch 2, dc in last dc: 68{76-84-92} ch-4 sps.

Row 4: Ch 4 and through◌ in each ch-4 sp last dc: 68{76-

Row 5: Ch 1, ch 4, (2 sc in next Shell, ch 4) across, sc in next ch-1 sp and in last dc: 69{77-85-93} ch-4 sps.

Row 6: Ch 3, turn; work Shell in each ch-4 sp across, skip next sc, dc in last sc: 69{77-85-93} Shells.

Row 7: Ch 5, turn; 2 dc in next Shell, (ch 4, 2 dc in next Shell) across, ch 2, dc in last dc: 68{76-84-92} ch-4 sps.

Row 8: Ch 4, turn; 2 dc in next ch-2 sp, work Shell in each ch-4 sp across, 2 dc in next ch-2 sp, ch 1, dc in last dc: 68{76-84-92} Shells.

Row 9: Ch 1, turn; sc in first dc and in next ch-1 sp, ch 4, (2 sc in next Shell, ch 4) across, sc in next ch-1 sp and in last dc: 69{77-85-93} ch-4 sps.

Rows 10-49: Repeat Rows 2-9, 5 times; do **not** finish off: 69{77-85-93} ch-4 sps.

RIGHT FRONT
Row 1: Ch 3, turn; work Shell in next 15{17-19-21} ch-4 sps, skip next sc, dc in next sc, leave remaining 54{60-66-72} ch-4 sps unworked: 15{17-19-21} Shells.

Row 2: Ch 5, turn; 2 sc in next Shell, (ch 4, 2 sc in next Shell) across, ch 2, dc in last dc: 14{16-18-20} ch-4 sps.

Row 3: Ch 4, turn; 2 dc in next ch-2 sp, work Shell in each ch-4 sp across, 2 dc in next ch-2 sp, ch 1, dc in last dc: 14{16-18-20} Shells.

Row 4: Ch 1, turn; sc in first dc and in next ch-1 sp, ch 4, (2 sc in next Shell, ch 4) across, sc in next ch-1 sp and in last dc: 15{17-19-21} ch-4 sps.

Row 5: Ch 3, turn; work Shell in each ch-4 sp across, skip next sc, dc in last sc: 15{17-19-21} Shells.

Row 6: Ch 5, turn; 2 dc in next Shell, (ch 4, 2 dc in next Shell) across, ch 2, dc in last dc: 14{16-18-20} ch-4 sps.

Row 7: Ch 4, turn; 2 dc in next ch-2 sp, work Shell in each ch-4 sp across, 2 dc in next ch-2 sp, ch 1, dc in last dc: 14{16-18-20} Shells.

Row 8: Ch 1, turn; sc in first dc and in next ch-1 sp, ch 4, (2 sc in next Shell, ch 4) across, sc in next ch-1 sp and in last dc: 15{17-19-21} ch-4 sps.

Row 9: Ch 3, turn; work Shell in each ch-4 sp across, skip next sc, dc in last sc: 15{17-19-21} Shells.

Rows 10 thru 22{22-30-30}: Repeat Rows 2-9, 1{1-2-2} time(s); then repeat Rows 2-6 once **more**; do **not** finish off: 14{16-18-20} ch-4 sps.

Continued on page 5.

1

4

NECK SHAPING

Row 1: Ch 1, turn; sc in first dc, sc in next ch-2 sp and in next 2 dc, (3 sc in next ch-4 sp, sc in next 2 dc) 2{2-3-3} times, (2 sc, ch 1, dc) in next ch-4 sp, work Shell in each ch-4 sp across, 2 dc in next ch-2 sp, ch 1, dc in last dc: 11{13-14-16} Shells.

Row 2: Ch 1, turn; sc in first dc and in next ch-1 sp, (ch 4, 2 sc in next Shell) across, ch 1, dc in last dc, leave remaining sts unworked: 11{13-14-16} ch-4 sps.

Row 3: Ch 2, turn; dc in next ch-1 sp, work Shell in each ch-4 sp across, skip next sc, dc in last sc: 11{13-14-16} Shells.

Row 4: Ch 5, turn; 2 sc in next Shell, (ch 4, 2 sc in next Shell) across, ch 1, dc in last dc: 10{12-13-15} ch-4 sps.

Row 5: Ch 2, turn; dc in next ch-1 sp, work Shell in each ch-4 sp across, 2 dc in next ch-2 sp, ch 1, dc in last dc: 10{12-13-15} Shells.

Row 6: Ch 1, turn; sc in first dc and in next ch-1 sp, (ch 4, 2 sc in next Shell) across, ch 1, dc in last dc: 10{12-13-15} ch-4 sps.

Row 7: Ch 2, turn; dc in next ch-1 sp, work Shell in each ch-4 sp across, skip next sc, dc in last sc: 10{12-13-15} Shells.

Row 8: Ch 5, turn; 2 dc in next Shell, (ch 4, 2 dc in next Shell) across, ch 1, sc in last dc: 9{11-12-14} ch-4 sps.

Row 9: Ch 2, turn; dc in next ch-1 sp, work Shell in each ch-4 sp across, 2 dc in next ch-2 sp, ch 1, dc in last dc: 9{11-12-14} Shells.

Row 10: Ch 1, turn; sc in first dc and in next ch-1 sp, (ch 4, 2 sc in next Shell) across, ch 1, dc in last dc: 9{11-12-14} ch-4 sps.

Row 11: Ch 2, turn; dc in next ch-1 sp, work Shell in each ch-4 sp across, skip next sc, dc in last sc: 9{11-12-14} Shells.

FOR SIZES SMALL, MEDIUM, AND EX-LARGE ONLY

Work same as Right Front for 4{6-0-2} rows, beginning by working Row 2: 9{10-0-13} Shells.

ALL SIZES

Last Row: Ch 1, turn; work 40{50-54-63} sc evenly spaced across; finish off.

BACK

Row 1: With **right** side facing, skip next 4 ch-4 sps from Right Front and join thread with slip st in next sc; ch 3, work Shell in next 31{35-39-43} ch-4 sps, skip next sc, dc in next sc, leave remaining 19{21-23-25} ch-4 sps unworked: 31{35-39-43} Shells.

Row 2: Ch 5, turn; 2 sc in next Shell, (ch 4, 2 sc in next Shell) across, ch 2, dc in last dc: 30{34-38-42} ch-4 sps.

Row 3: Ch 4, turn; 2 dc in next ch-2 sp, work Shell in each ch-4 sp across, 2 dc in next ch-2 sp, ch 1, dc in last dc: 30{34-38-42} Shells.

Row 4: Ch 1, turn; sc in first dc and in next ch-1 sp, ch 4, (2 sc in next Shell, ch 4) across, sc in next ch-1 sp and in last dc: 31{35-39-43} ch-4 sps.

Row 5: Ch 3, turn; work Shell in each ch-4 sp across, skip next sc, dc in last sc: 31{35-39-43} Shells.

Row 6: Ch 5, turn; 2 dc in next Shell, (ch 4, 2 dc in next Shell) across, ch 2, dc in last dc: 30{34-38-42} ch-4 sps.

Row 7: Ch 4, turn; 2 dc in next ch-2 sp, work Shell in each ch-4 sp across, 2 dc in next ch-2 sp, ch 1, dc in last dc: 30{34-38-42} Shells.

Row 8: Ch 1, turn; sc in first dc and in next ch-1 sp, ch 4, (2 sc in next Shell, ch 4) across, sc in next ch-1 sp and in last dc: 31{35-39-43} ch-4 sps.

Row 9: Ch 3, turn; work Shell in each ch-4 sp across, skip next sc, dc in last sc: 31{35-39-43} Shells.

Rows 10 thru 37{39-41-43}: Repeat Rows 2-9, 3{3-3-4} times; then repeat Rows 2 thru 5{7-9-3} once **more**; do **not** finish off: 31{34-39-42} Shells.

Row 38{40-42-44}: Ch 1, turn; work 138{158-176-194} sc evenly spaced across; finish off.

LEFT FRONT

Row 1: With **right** side facing, skip next 4 ch-4 sps from Back and join thread with slip st in next sc; ch 3, work Shell in each ch-4 sp across, skip next sc, dc in last sc: 15{17-19-21} Shells.

Row 2: Ch 5, turn; 2 sc in next Shell, (ch 4, 2 sc in next Shell) across, ch 2, dc in last dc: 14{16-18-20} ch-4 sps.

Row 3: Ch 4, turn; 2 dc in next ch-2 sp, work Shell in each ch-4 sp across, 2 dc in next ch-2 sp, ch 1, dc in last dc: 14{16-18-20} Shells.

Row 4: Ch 1, turn; sc in first dc and in next ch-1 sp, ch 4, (2 sc in next Shell, ch 4) across, sc in next ch-1 sp and in last dc: 15{17-19-21} ch-4 sps.

Row 5: Ch 3, turn; work Shell in each ch-4 sp across, skip next sc, dc in last sc: 15{17-19-21} Shells.

Row 6: Ch 5, turn; 2 dc in next Shell, (ch 4, 2 dc in next Shell) across, ch 2, dc in last dc: 14{16-18-20} ch-4 sps.

Row 7: Ch 4, turn; 2 dc in next ch-2 sp, work Shell in each ch-4 sp across, 2 dc in next ch-2 sp, ch 1, dc in last dc: 14{16-18-20} Shells.

Row 8: Ch 1, turn; sc in first dc and in next ch-1 sp, ch 4, (2 sc in next Shell, ch 4) across, sc in next ch-1 sp and in last dc: 15{17-19-21} ch-4 sps.

Row 9: Ch 3, turn; work Shell in each ch-4 sp across, skip next sc, dc in last sc: 15{17-19-21} Shells.

Rows 10 thru 22{22-30-30}: Repeat Rows 2-9, 1{1-2-2} time(s); then repeat Rows 2-6 once **more**; do **not** finish off: 14{16-18-20} ch-4 sps.

NECK SHAPING

Row 1: Ch 4, turn; 2 dc in next ch-2 sp, work Shell in next 11{13-14-16} ch-4 sps, (dc, ch 1, 2 sc) in next ch-4 sp, sc in next 2 dc, (3 sc in next ch-4 sp, sc in next 2 dc) 2{2-3-3} times, sc in next ch-2 sp and in last dc: 11{13-14-16} Shells.

Row 2: Turn; slip st in first 16{16-21-21} sc and in next ch, slip st in next dc, ch 4, (2 sc in next Shell, ch 4) across, sc in next ch-1 sp and in last dc: 11{13-14-16} ch-4 sps.

Row 3: Ch 3, turn; work Shell in each ch-4 sp across, skip next 2 sc, decrease: 11{13-14-16} Shells.

Row 4: Ch 4, turn; 2 sc in next Shell, (ch 4, 2 sc in next Shell) across, ch 2, dc in last dc: 10{12-13-15} ch-4 sps.

Row 5: Ch 4, turn; 2 dc in first ch-2 sp, work Shell in each ch-4 sp across, skip next 2 sc, decrease: 10{12-13-15} Shells.

Row 6: Ch 4, turn; (2 sc in next Shell, ch 4) across, sc in next ch-1 sp and in last dc: 10{12-13-15} ch-4 sps.

Row 7: Ch 3, turn; work Shell in each ch-4 sp across, skip next 2 sc, decrease: 10{12-13-15} Shells.

Row 8: Ch 1, turn; sc in first dc, ch 1, 2 dc in next Shell, (ch 4, 2 dc in next Shell) across, ch 2, dc in last dc: 9{11-12-14} ch-4 sps.

Row 9: Ch 4, turn; 2 dc in next ch-2 sp, work Shell in each ch-4 sp across, skip next 2 dc, decrease: 9{11-12-14} Shells.

Row 10: Ch 4, turn; (2 sc in next Shell, ch 4) across, sc in next ch-1 sp and in last dc: 9{11-12-14} ch-4 sps.

Row 11: Ch 3, turn; work Shell in each ch-4 sp across, skip next 2 sc, decrease: 9{11-12-14} Shells.

FOR SIZES SMALL, MEDIUM, AND EX-LARGE ONLY

Work same as Left Front for 4{6-0-2} rows, beginning by working Row 2: 9{10-0-13} Shells.

ALL SIZES

Last Row: Ch 1, turn; work 40{50-54-63} sc evenly spaced across; finish off.

SLEEVE (Make 2)

Ch 99{111-99-111}.

Row 1: Sc in second ch from hook and in next ch, ★ ch 4, skip next 4 chs, sc in next 2 chs; repeat from ★ across: 16{18-16-18} ch-4 sps.

Row 2 (Right side)**:** Ch 3, turn; dc in next sc, work Shell in each ch-4 sp across, dc in last 2 sc: 16{18-16-18} Shells.

Note: Mark Row 2 as **right** side.

Row 3: Ch 1, turn; sc in first 2 dc, ch 4, (2 sc in next Shell, ch 4) across, sc in last 2 dc: 17{19-17-19} ch-4 sps.

Rows 4-6: Repeat Rows 2 and 3 once, then repeat Row 2 once **more**: 18{20-18-20} Shells.

Row 7: Ch 3, turn; dc in next dc, ch 4, (2 dc in next Shell, ch 4) across, dc in last 2 dc: 19{21-19-21} ch-4 sps.

Row 8: Ch 3, turn; dc in next dc, work Shell in each ch-4 sp across, dc in last 2 dc: 19{21-19-21} Shells.

Row 9: Ch 1, turn; sc in first 2 dc, ch 4, (2 sc in next Shell, ch 4) across, sc in last 2 dc: 20{22-20-22} ch-4 sps.

Rows 10 thru 41{41-49-49}: Repeat Rows 2-9, 4{4-5-5} times: 36{38-40-42} ch-4 sps.

Row 42{42-50-50}: Ch 3, turn; work Shell in each ch-4 sp across, skip next sc, dc in last sc: 36{38-40-42} Shells.

Row 43{43-51-51}: Ch 5, turn; 2 sc in next Shell, (ch 4, 2 sc in next Shell) across, ch 2, dc in last dc: 35{37-39-41} ch-4 sps.

Row 44{44-52-52}: Ch 4, turn; 2 dc in next ch-2 sp, work Shell in each ch-4 sp across, 2 dc in next ch-2 sp, ch 1, dc in last dc: 35{37-39-41} Shells.

Row 45{45-53-53}: Ch 1, turn; sc in first dc and in next ch-1 sp, ch 4, (2 sc in next Shell, ch 4) across, sc in next ch-1 sp and in last dc: 36{38-40-42} ch-4 sps.

Row 46{46-54-54}: Ch 3, turn; work Shell in each ch-4 sp across, skip next sc, dc in last sc: 36{38-40-42} Shells.

Row 47{47-55-55}: Ch 5, turn; 2 dc in next Shell, (ch 4, 2 dc in next Shell) across, ch 2, dc in last dc: 35{37-39-41} ch-4 sps.

Row 48{48-56-56}: Ch 4, turn; 2 dc in next ch-2 sp, work Shell in each ch-4 sp across, 2 dc in next ch-2 sp, ch 1, dc in last dc: 35{37-39-41} Shells.

Row 49{49-57-57}: Ch 1, turn; sc in first dc and in next ch-1 sp, ch 4, (2 sc in next Shell, ch 4) across, sc in next ch-1 sp and in last dc: 36{38-40-42} ch-4 sps.

Repeat Rows 42{42-50-50} thru 49{49-57-57} until Sleeve measures approximately 17{17½-18½-19}" from beginning ch, ending by working a **right** side row; do **not** finish off.

Last Row: Ch 1, turn; work 162{170-180-190} sc evenly spaced across; finish off.

FINISHING

Sew shoulder seams.

Sew last row on Sleeve to end of rows along armhole edge, matching center of Sleeve to shoulder seam; sew unworked sts of armhole to end of rows on Sleeve.

Weave Sleeve seam *(Fig. 3, page 1)*.

SLEEVE EDGING

With **right** side facing and working in sps across beginning ch, join thread with slip st in first ch-4 sp; ch 3, (dc, ch 2, 2 dc) in same sp, work Shell in next ch-4 sp and in each ch-4 sp around; join with slip st to first dc, finish off: 16{18-16-18} Shells.

Repeat for second Sleeve.

Continued on page 9.

3

BOTTOM EDGING

With **right** side facing, join thread with slip st in free loop of ch at base of first sc *(Fig. 2, page 1)*; ch 3, work Shell in each ch-4 sp across, skip next ch, dc in free loop of last ch; do **not** finish off: 69{77-85-93} Shells.

RIGHT FRONT EDGING

Row 1: Ch 1, work 150{150-165-165} sc evenly spaced across end of rows ending in Row 1 of Neck Shaping.

Rows 2 and 3: Ch 1, turn; sc in each sc across.

Row 4 (Buttonhole row): Ch 3, turn; dc in next 2 sc, ch 3, ★ skip next 3 sc, dc in next 25{25-28-28} sc, ch 3; repeat from ★ across to last 7 sc, skip next 3 sc, dc in last 4 sc: 6 ch-3 sps.

Row 5: Ch 1, turn; sc in each dc across working 3 sc in each ch-3 sp.

Rows 6 and 7: Ch 1, turn; sc in each sc across.

Finish off.

LEFT FRONT EDGING

Row 1: With **right** side facing, join thread with slip st in end of Row 1 of Neck Shaping; ch 1, work 150{150-165-165} sc evenly spaced across end of rows.

Rows 2 and 3: Ch 1, turn; sc in each sc across.

Row 4: Ch 3, turn; dc in next sc and in each sc across.

Row 5: Ch 1, turn; sc in each dc across.

Rows 6 and 7: Ch 1, turn; sc in each sc across.

Finish off.

COLLAR

Row 1: With **right** side facing, join thread with slip st in end of Row 4 of Right Front Edging; ch 1, work 4 sc across end of rows, sc in next 16{16-21-21} sc, work 32{38-29-29} sc evenly spaced along end of rows of neck edge, sc in each sc across Back, work 32{38-29-29} sc evenly spaced along neck edge, sc in next 16{16-21-21} sc, work 4 sc across end of rows ending in Row 4 of Left Neck Edging: 162{174-176-176} sc.

Row 2: Ch 3, turn; dc in next sc, (ch 4, skip next 4 sc, dc in next 2 sc) 2{3-4-4} times, (ch 4, skip next 2 sc, dc in next 2 sc) 11{11-9-9} times, (ch 4, skip next 4 sc, dc in next 2 sc) 8{8-9-9} times, (ch 4, skip next 2 sc, dc in next 2 sc) 11{11-9-9} times, (ch 4, skip next 4 sc, dc in next 2 sc) 2{3-4-4} times: 34{36-35-35} ch-4 sps.

Row 3: Ch 3, turn; work Shell in each ch-4 sp across, skip next dc, dc in last dc: 34{36-35-35} Shells.

Row 4: Ch 5, turn; 2 sc in next Shell, (ch 4, 2 sc in next Shell) across, ch 2, dc in last dc: 33{35-34-34} ch-4 sps.

Row 5: Ch 4, turn; 2 dc in next ch-2 sp, work Shell in each ch-4 sp across, 2 dc in next ch-2 sp, ch 1, dc in last dc: 33{35-34-34} Shells.

Row 6: Ch 1, turn; sc in first dc and in next ch-1 sp, ch 4, (2 sc in next Shell, ch 4) across, sc in next ch-1 sp and in last dc: 34{36-35-35} ch-4 sps.

Row 7: Ch 3, turn; work Shell in each ch-4 sp across, skip next sc, dc in last sc: 34{36-35-35} Shells.

Row 8: Ch 5, turn; 2 dc in next Shell, (ch 4, 2 dc in next Shell) across, ch 2, dc in last dc: 33{35-34-34} ch-4 sps.

Row 9: Ch 4, turn; 2 dc in next ch-2 sp, work Shell in each ch-4 sp across, 2 dc in next ch-2 sp, ch 1, dc in last dc: 33{35-34-34} Shells.

Row 10: Ch 3, turn; dc in next ch-1 sp, ch 4, (2 dc in next Shell, ch 4) across, dc in next ch-1 sp and in last dc: 34{36-35-35} ch-4 sps.

Row 11: Ch 3, turn; work Shell in each ch-4 sp across, skip next dc, dc in last dc; finish off.

Sew buttons opposite buttonholes.

---

2. V-NECK PULLOVER

Size:	Small	Medium	Large	Ex-Large
Chest				
Measurement:	32-34"	36-38"	40-42"	44-46"
Finished Chest				
Measurement:	36"	40"	44"	48"

Size Note: Instructions are written for size Small with sizes Medium, Large, and Ex-Large in braces { }. Instructions will be easier to read if you circle all the numbers pertaining to your size. If only one number is given, it applies to all sizes.

MATERIALS

Bedspread Weight Cotton Thread (size 10):
2,360{2,680-3,050-3,350} yards
Steel crochet hook, size 8 (1.50 mm) **or** size needed for gauge
Tapestry needle

GAUGE: In pattern, 36 dc and 15 rows = 4"

Gauge Swatch: 3"w x 4"h
Ch 29.
Row 1: Dc in fourth ch from hook **(3 skipped chs count as first dc)** and in each ch across: 27 dc.
Row 2: Ch 4 **(counts as first dc plus ch 1)**, turn; skip next dc, dc in next dc, ★ ch 1, skip next dc, dc in next dc; repeat from ★ across: 14 dc and 13 ch-1 sps.
Row 3: Ch 3 **(counts as first dc)**, turn; dc in each ch-1 sp and in each dc across: 27 dc.
Rows 4-15: Repeat Rows 2 and 3, 6 times.
Finish off.

Pullover is worked in one piece to armhole.

9

STITCH GUIDE

TREBLE CROCHET *(abbreviated tr)*
YO twice, insert hook in st indicated, YO and pull up a loop (4 loops on hook), (YO and draw through 2 loops on hook) 3 times.

DECREASE
★ YO, insert hook in **next** st or ch-1 sp, YO and pull up a loop, YO and draw through 2 loops on hook; repeat from ★ once **more**, YO and draw through all 3 loops on hook **(counts as one dc)**.

PICOT
Ch 3, sc in top of dc just made.

CLUSTER
† YO, insert hook in end of next row, YO and pull up a loop, YO and draw through 2 loops on hook, YO, insert hook in end of same row, YO and pull up a loop, YO and draw through 2 loops on hook †, (YO, insert hook in **next** marked dc of Front, YO and pull up a loop, YO and draw through 2 loops on hook) 3 times, repeat from † to † once, YO and draw through all 8 loops on hook.

BODY

Ch 324{364-396-436}; being careful not to twist ch, join with slip st to form a ring.

Rnd 1 (Right side)**:** Ch 3 **(counts as first dc, now and throughout)**, dc in next ch and in each ch around; join with slip st to first dc: 324{364-396-436} dc.

Note: Loop a short piece of thread around any stitch to mark Rnd 1 as **right** side.

Rnd 2: Ch 4 **(counts as first dc plus ch 1, now and throughout)**, turn; skip next dc, ★ dc in next dc, ch 1, skip next dc; repeat from ★ around; join with slip st to first dc: 162{182-198-218} ch-1 sps.

Rnd 3: Ch 3, turn; dc in each ch-1 sp and in each dc around; join with slip st to first dc: 324{364-396-436} dc.

Repeat Rnds 2 and 3 until Body measures approximately 14{14½-15-15½}" from beginning ch, ending by working Rnd 3; do **not** finish off.

BACK

Row 1: Turn; slip st in next 8 dc, ch 4, skip next dc, dc in next dc, ★ ch 1, skip next dc, dc in next dc; repeat from ★ 70{80-88-98} times **more**, leave remaining dc unworked: 72{82-90-100} ch-1 sps.

Row 2: Ch 3, turn; dc in each ch-1 sp and in each dc across: 145{165-181-201} dc.

Row 3: Ch 4, turn; skip next dc, dc in next dc, ★ ch 1, skip next dc, dc in next dc; repeat from ★ across: 72{82-90-100} ch-1 sps.

Rows 4 thru 34{36-38-40}: Repeat Rows 2 and 3, 15{16-17-18} times; then repeat Row 2 once **more**.

Finish off.

RIGHT FRONT

Row 1: With **wrong** side facing, skip next 17 dc from Back and join thread with slip st in next dc; ch 4, ★ skip next dc, dc in next dc, ch 1; repeat from ★ 33{38-42-47} times **more**, skip next dc, decrease, place markers in last st worked into and in next 2 dc for st placement, leave remaining 90{100-108-118} dc unworked: 35{40-44-49} ch-1 sps.

Row 2 (Decrease row)**:** Ch 2, turn; dc in next ch-1 sp and in each dc and each ch-1 sp across: 70{80-88-98} dc.

Row 3 (Decrease row)**:** Ch 4, turn; ★ skip next dc, dc in next dc, ch 1; repeat from ★ across to last 3 dc, skip next dc, decrease: 34{39-43-48} ch-1 sps.

Rows 4 thru 24{26-28-30}: Repeat Rows 2 and 3, 10{11-12-13} times; then repeat Row 2 once **more**: 48{56-62-70} dc.

Row 25{27-29-31}: Ch 4, turn; ★ skip next dc, dc in next dc, ch 1; repeat from ★ across to last 3 dc, skip next dc, dc in last 2 dc: 23{27-30-34} ch-1 sps.

Row 26{28-30-32}: Ch 2, turn; dc in next dc and in each ch-1 sp and each dc across: 47{55-61-69} dc.

Row 27{29-31-33}: Ch 4, turn; skip next dc, dc in next dc, ★ ch 1, skip next dc, dc in next dc; repeat from ★ across: 23{27-30-34} ch-1 sps.

Row 28{30-32-34}: Ch 2, turn; dc in next ch-1 sp and in each dc and each ch-1 sp across: 46{54-60-68} dc.

Rows 29{31-33-35} and 30{32-34-36}: Repeat Rows 25{27-29-31} and 26{28-30-32}: 45{53-59-67} dc.

Row 31{33-35-37}: Ch 4, turn; skip next dc, dc in next dc, ★ ch 1, skip next dc, dc in next dc; repeat from ★ across: 22{26-29-33} ch-1 sps.

Row 32{34-36-38}: Ch 3, turn; dc in next ch-1 sp and in each dc across: 45{53-59-67} dc.

Rows 33{35-37-39} and 34{36-38-40}: Repeat Rows 31{33-35-37} and 32{34-36-38}.

Finish off.

LEFT FRONT

Row 1: With **wrong** side facing, skip next dc from Right Front and join thread with slip st in next dc (third marked dc, do **not** remove marker); ch 2, dc in next dc, ★ ch 1, skip next dc, dc in next dc; repeat from ★ 34{39-43-48} times **more**, leave remaining 17 dc unworked: 35{40-44-49} ch-1 sps.

Row 2 (Decrease row)**:** Ch 3, turn; dc in each ch-1 sp and in each dc across to last ch-1 sp, decrease: 70{80-88-98} dc.

Row 3 (Decrease row)**:** Ch 2, turn; dc in next dc, ★ ch 1, skip next dc, dc in next dc; repeat from ★ across; do **not** finish off: 34{39-43-48} ch-1 sps.

Continued on page 11.

Rows 4 thru 24{26-28-30}: Repeat Rows 2 and 3, 10{11-12-13} times; then repeat Row 2 once **more**: 48{56-62-70} dc.

Row 25{27-29-31}: Ch 3, turn; dc in next dc, ★ ch 1, skip next dc, dc in next dc; repeat from ★ across: 23{27-30-34} ch-1 sps.

Row 26{28-30-32}: Ch 3, turn; dc in each ch-1 sp and in each dc across to last 2 dc, decrease: 47{55-61-69} dc.

Row 27{29-31-33}: Ch 4, turn; skip next dc, dc in next dc, ★ ch 1, skip next dc, dc in next dc; repeat from ★ across: 23{27-30-34} ch-1 sps.

Row 28{30-32-34}: Ch 3, turn; dc in each ch-1 sp and in each dc across to last ch-1 sp, decrease: 46{54-60-68} dc.

Rows 29{31-33-35} and 30{32-34-36}: Repeat Rows 25{27-29-31} and 26{28-30-32}: 45{53-59-67} dc.

Row 31{33-35-37}: Ch 4, turn; skip next dc, dc in next dc, ★ ch 1, skip next dc, dc in next dc; repeat from ★ across: 22{26-29-33} ch-1 sps.

Row 32{34-36-38}: Ch 3, turn; dc in each ch-1 sp and in each dc across: 45{53-59-67} dc.

Rows 33{35-37-39} and 34{36-38-40}: Repeat Rows 31{33-35-37} and 32{34-36-38}.

Finish off.

SLEEVE (Make 2)
Ch 69{81-87-87}.

Row 1 (Right side)**:** Dc in fourth ch from hook and in each ch across: 67{79-85-85} dc.

Note: Mark Row 1 as **right** side.

Row 2 (Increase row)**:** Ch 5 **(counts as first tr plus ch 1)**, turn; dc in same st, ch 1, ★ skip next dc, dc in next dc, ch 1; repeat from ★ across to last 2 dc, skip next dc, (dc, ch 1, tr) in last dc: 35{41-44-44} ch-1 sps.

Row 3: Ch 3, turn; dc in each ch-1 sp and in each st across: 71{83-89-89} dc.

Rows 4 thru 43{37-37-43}: Repeat Rows 2 and 3, 20{17-17-20} times: 151{151-157-169} dc.

Row 44{38-38-44}: Ch 4, turn; skip next dc, dc in next dc, ★ ch 1, skip next dc, dc in next dc; repeat from ★ across: 75{75-78-84} ch-1 sps.

Row 45{39-39-45}: Ch 3, turn; dc in each ch-1 sp and in each st across: 151{151-157-169} dc.

Row 46{40-40-46}: Repeat Row 2: 77{77-80-86} ch-1 sps.

Maintaining pattern, increase in same manner every fourth row, 2{4-5-4} times **more**: 81{85-90-94} ch-1 sps.

Work even for 9 rows: 163{171-181-189} dc.

Finish off.

FINISHING
Sew shoulder seams.

Sew last row on Sleeve to end of rows along armhole edge, matching center of Sleeve to shoulder seam; sew unworked sts of armhole to end of rows on Sleeve.

Weave Sleeve seams *(Fig. 3, page 1)*.

BOTTOM EDGING
Rnd 1: With **right** side facing and working in free loops of beginning ch *(Fig. 2, page 1)*, join thread with slip st in first ch; ch 4, skip next 1{0-1-0} ch *(see Zeros, page 1)*, dc in next ch, ch 1, ★ skip next ch, dc in next ch, ch 1; repeat from ★ around to last 1{0-1-0} ch, skip last 1{0-1-0} ch; join with slip st to first dc: 162{183-198-219} ch-1 sps.

Rnd 2: Do **not** turn; slip st in first ch-1 sp, ch 1, sc in same sp, dc in next ch-1 sp, (work Picot, dc in same sp) 4 times, ★ sc in next 2 ch-1 sps, dc in next ch-1 sp, (work Picot, dc in same sp) 4 times; repeat from ★ around to last ch-1 sp, sc in last ch-1 sp; join with slip st to first sc, finish off.

SLEEVE EDGING
Rnd 1: With **right** side facing and working in free loops of beginning ch, join thread with slip st in first ch; ch 4, ★ skip next ch, dc in next ch, ch 1; repeat from ★ around to last 2 chs, skip last 2 chs; join with slip st to first dc: 33{39-42-42} ch-1 sps.

Rnd 2: Do **not** turn; slip st in first ch-1 sp, ch 1, sc in same sp, dc in next ch-1 sp, (work Picot, dc in same sp) 4 times, ★ sc in next 2 ch-1 sps, dc in next ch-1 sp, (work Picot, dc in same sp) 4 times; repeat from ★ around to last ch-1 sp, sc in last ch-1 sp; join with slip st to first sc, finish off.

Repeat for second Sleeve.

NECK EDGING
Rnd 1: With **right** side facing, join thread with slip st in first dc on Back neck edge; ch 3, dc in next 54{58-62-66} dc; 3 dc in end of each row across to last row, work Cluster, 3 dc in end of each row across; join with slip st to first dc: 254{270-286-302} sts.

Rnd 2: Do **not** turn; ch 4, (skip next dc, dc in next dc, ch 1) 74{79-84-89} times, ★ YO, skip next dc, insert hook in **next** st, YO and pull up a loop, YO and draw through 2 loops on hook; repeat from ★ 4 times **more**, YO and draw through all 6 loops on hook, place marker around st just made, ch 1, skip next dc, (dc in next dc, ch 1, skip next dc) across; join with slip st to first dc.

Rnd 3: Ch 3, dc in each ch-1 sp and in each dc across to within 2 dc of marked st, YO, insert hook in next dc, YO and pull up a loop, YO and draw through 2 loops on hook, ★ YO, skip next ch-1 sp, insert hook in **next** st, YO and pull up a loop, YO and draw through 2 loops on hook; repeat from ★ 3 times **more**, YO and draw through all 6 loops on hook, dc in each ch-1 sp and in each dc across; join with slip st to first dc, finish off.

3. V-NECK CARDIGAN

Size:	Small	Medium	Large	Ex-Large
Chest Measurement:	32-34"	36-38"	40-42"	44-46"
Finished Chest Measurement:	36½"	40"	44"	48"

Size Note: Instructions are written for size Small with sizes Medium, Large, and Ex-Large in braces { }. Instructions will be easier to read if you circle all the numbers pertaining to your size. If only one number is given, it applies to all sizes.

MATERIALS
Bedspread Weight Cotton Thread (size 10):
    2,255{2,630-2,985-3,400} yards
Steel crochet hook, size 8 (1.50 mm) **or** size needed
    for gauge
Tapestry needle
⅜" Buttons - 5
Sewing needle and thread

GAUGE: In pattern, (Cluster, ch 2) 10 times
        and 9 rows = 3"

Gauge Swatch: 3¼"w x 3"h
Ch 38.
Work same as Body for 9 rows.
Finish off.

Cardigan is worked in one piece to armhole.

STITCH GUIDE

TREBLE CROCHET *(abbreviated tr)*
YO twice, insert hook in st indicated, YO and pull up a loop (4 loops on hook), (YO and draw through 2 loops on hook) 3 times.

CLUSTER *(uses one st)*
★ YO, insert hook in st indicated, YO and pull up a loop, YO and draw through 2 loops on hook; repeat from ★ once **more**, YO and draw through all 3 loops on hook.

BODY
Ch 359{395-434-473}.

Row 1 (Right side): Work Cluster in eighth ch from hook, ch 2, ★ skip next 2 chs, work Cluster in next ch, ch 2; repeat from ★ across to last 3 chs, skip next 2 chs, dc in last ch: 117{129-142-155} Clusters.

Note: Loop a short piece of thread around any stitch to mark Row 1 as **right** side.

Row 2: Ch 5 **(counts as first dc plus ch 2, now and throughout)**, turn; (work Cluster in next Cluster, ch 2) across, skip next 2 chs, dc in next ch.

Row 3: Ch 5, turn; (work Cluster in next Cluster, ch 2) across, dc in last dc.

Repeat Row 3 until Body measures approximately 12{12½-13-13½}" from beginning ch, ending by working a **wrong** side row; do **not** finish off.

RIGHT FRONT
Row 1: Ch 5, turn; (work Cluster in next Cluster, ch 2) 24{27-31-34} times, dc in next Cluster, leave remaining 92{101-110-120} Clusters unworked: 24{27-31-34} Clusters.

Row 2: Ch 4 **(counts as first tr, now and throughout)**, turn; (work Cluster in next Cluster, ch 2) across, dc in last dc.

Row 3 (Decrease row): Ch 5, turn; (work Cluster in next Cluster, ch 2) across to last Cluster, dc in last Cluster, leave last tr unworked: 23{26-30-33} Clusters.

Row 4: Ch 4, turn; (work Cluster in next Cluster, ch 2) across, dc in last dc.

Row 5 (Decrease row): Ch 5, turn; work Cluster in next Cluster, (ch 2, work Cluster in next Cluster) across to last Cluster, dc in last Cluster, leave last tr unworked: 22{25-29-32} Clusters.

Row 6 (Decrease row): Ch 5, turn; skip first Cluster, (work Cluster in next Cluster, ch 2) across, dc in last dc: 21{24-28-31} Clusters.

FOR SIZES SMALL, MEDIUM, AND EX-LARGE ONLY
Rows 7 thru 10{10-0-8}: Ch 5, turn; (work Cluster in next Cluster, ch 2) across, dc in last dc.

ALL SIZES
Note: Place marker in last dc made for st placement.

Rows 11{11-7-9} thru 26{28-28-30}: Repeat Rows 2 and 3, 8{9-11-11} times: 13{15-17-20} Clusters.

Finish off.

BACK
Row 1: With **right** side facing, skip next 7 Clusters from Right Front and join thread with slip st in next Cluster; ch 5, (work Cluster in next Cluster, ch 2) 51{57-62-69} times, dc in next Cluster, leave remaining 32{35-39-42} Clusters unworked: 51{57-62-69} Clusters.

Row 2: Ch 4, turn; work Cluster in next Cluster, (ch 2, work Cluster in next Cluster) across, tr in last dc.

Row 3 (Decrease row): Ch 5, turn; skip first Cluster, (work Cluster in next Cluster, ch 2) across to last Cluster, dc in last Cluster, leave last tr unworked: 49{55-60-67} Clusters.

Row 4: Ch 4, turn; work Cluster in next Cluster, (ch 2, work Cluster in next Cluster) across, tr in last dc.

Row 5 (Decrease row): Ch 3, turn; skip first Cluster, work Cluster in next Cluster, (ch 2, work Cluster in next Cluster) across to last Cluster, dc in last Cluster, leave last tr unworked; do **not** finish off: 47{53-58-65} Clusters.

Continued on page 13.

Row 6 (Decrease row)**:** Ch 5, turn; skip first Cluster, (work Cluster in next Cluster, ch 2) across to last Cluster, dc in last Cluster, leave last st unworked: 45{51-56-63} Clusters.

Rows 7 thru 26{28-28-30}: Ch 5, turn; (work Cluster in next Cluster, ch 2) across, dc in last dc.

Finish off.

LEFT FRONT

Row 1: With **right** side facing, skip next 7 Clusters from Back and join thread with slip st in next Cluster; ch 5, (work Cluster in next Cluster, ch 2) across, dc in last dc: 24{27-31-34} Clusters.

Row 2: Ch 5, turn; work Cluster in next Cluster, (ch 2, work Cluster in next Cluster) across, tr in last dc.

Row 3 (Decrease row)**:** Ch 5, turn; skip first Cluster, (work Cluster in next Cluster, ch 2) across, dc in last dc: 23{26-30-33} Clusters.

Row 4: Ch 5, turn; work Cluster in next Cluster, (ch 2, work Cluster in next Cluster) across, tr in last dc.

Row 5 (Decrease row)**:** Ch 3, turn; skip first Cluster, (work Cluster in next Cluster, ch 2) across, dc in last dc: 22{25-29-32} Clusters.

Row 6 (Decrease row)**:** Ch 5, turn; (work Cluster in next Cluster, ch 2) across to last Cluster, skip last Cluster, dc in last st: 21{24-28-31} Clusters.

FOR SIZES SMALL, MEDIUM, AND EX-LARGE ONLY

Rows 7 thru 10{10-0-8}: Ch 5, turn; (work Cluster in next Cluster, ch 2) across, dc in last dc.

ALL SIZES

Note: Place marker in first dc made on last row for st placement.

Rows 11{11-7-9} thru 26{28-28-30}: Repeat Rows 2 and 3, 8{9-11-11} times: 13{15-17-20} Clusters.

Finish off.

SLEEVE (Make 2)
BODY

Ch 72{84-90-96}; being careful not to twist ch, join with slip st to form a ring.

Rnd 1 (Right side)**:** [Ch 2, dc in same st (**first Cluster made**)], ch 2, skip next 2 chs, ★ work Cluster in next ch, ch 2, skip next 2 chs; repeat from ★ around; join with slip st to first dc: 24{28-30-32} Clusters.

*Note: Mark Rnd 1 as **right** side.*

Rnd 2 (Increase rnd)**:** Ch 2, turn; dc in same st, ch 2, (work Cluster, ch 2) twice in next Cluster, (work Cluster in next Cluster, ch 2) around to last Cluster, (work Cluster, ch 2) twice in last Cluster; join with slip st to first dc: 26{30-32-34} Clusters.

Rnds 3-5: Ch 2, turn; dc in same st, ch 2, (work Cluster in next Cluster, ch 2) around; join with slip st to first dc.

Rnd 6 (Increase rnd)**:** Ch 2, turn; dc in same st, ch 2, (work Cluster, ch 2) twice in next Cluster, (work Cluster in next Cluster, ch 2) around to last Cluster, (work Cluster, ch 2) twice in last Cluster; join with slip st to first dc: 28{32-34-36} Clusters.

Maintaining pattern, continue to increase every fourth rnd, 2{1-3-5} time(s) **more**; then increase every sixth rnd, 5{6-5-4} times: 42{46-50-54} Clusters.

Work even until Sleeve measures approximately 17{17½-18-18½}" from beginning ch, ending by working a **wrong** side rnd; do **not** finish off.

SLEEVE CAP

Row 1: Turn; (slip st in next 2 chs and in next Cluster) 4 times, ch 5, (work Cluster in next Cluster, ch 2) 33{37-41-45} times, dc in next Cluster, leave remaining Clusters unworked: 33{37-41-45} Clusters.

Row 2: Ch 4, turn; work Cluster in next Cluster, (ch 2, work Cluster in next Cluster) across, tr in last dc.

Row 3 (Decrease row)**:** Ch 5, turn; skip first Cluster, (work Cluster in next Cluster, ch 2) across to last Cluster, dc in last Cluster, leave last tr unworked: 31{35-39-43} Clusters.

Row 4: Ch 4, turn; work Cluster in next Cluster, (ch 2, work Cluster in next Cluster) across, tr in last dc.

Rows 5 and 6: Repeat Rows 3 and 4: 29{33-37-41} Clusters.

Rows 7 thru 17{19-21-23}: Ch 4, turn; skip first Cluster, work Cluster in next Cluster, (ch 2, work Cluster in next Cluster) across to last Cluster, tr in last Cluster, leave last tr unworked: 7 Clusters.

Finish off.

FINISHING

Sew shoulder seams.

Set in Sleeves matching center of Sleeve to shoulder seam *(Fig. 3, page 1)*.

SLEEVE RUFFLE

Rnd 1: With **right** side facing and working in sps and in free loops of beginning ch *(Fig. 2, page 1)*, join thread with slip st in ch at base of first Cluster; ch 1, work 72{84-92-96} sc evenly spaced around; join with slip st to first sc.

Rnd 2: Ch 1, do **not** turn; sc in same st, ch 4, skip next 3 sc, ★ sc in next sc, ch 4, skip next 3 sc; repeat from ★ around; join with slip st to first sc: 18{21-23-24} ch-4 sps.

Rnd 3: Slip st in first ch-4 sp, ch 3 (**counts as first dc, now and throughout**), 6 dc in same sp, 7 dc in each ch-4 sp around; join with slip st to first dc.

Rnd 4: Ch 3, dc in next dc and in each dc around; join with slip st to first dc.

Rnd 5: Ch 1, sc in same st, ch 3, (sc in next dc, ch 3) around; join with slip st to first sc, finish off.

Repeat for second Sleeve.

BODY EDGING
Row 1: With **right** side facing and working in end of rows across Right Front, join thread with slip st in first row; ch 1, work 138{144-138-144} sc evenly spaced across to first marker, remove marker and place in last sc made; sc evenly across Right Front neck edge, 2 sc in next ch-2 sp on Back, (sc in next Cluster, 2 sc in next ch-2 sp) across, sc evenly across Left Front neck edge to next marker, sc in end of next row, remove marker and place in sc just made, work 137{143-137-143} sc evenly spaced across Left Front.

Row 2: Ch 1, turn; ★ sc in each sc across to next marked sc, (sc, ch 1, sc) in marked sc; repeat from ★ once **more**, sc in each sc across.

Row 3: Ch 1, turn; ★ sc in each sc across to next ch-1 sp, sc in ch-1 sp, place marker in sc just made; repeat from ★ once **more**, sc in each sc across.

Row 4 (Buttonhole row)**:** Ch 1, turn; ★ sc in each sc across to next marked sc, (sc, ch 1, sc) in marked sc; repeat from ★ once **more**, sc in next 3 sc, ch 3, skip next 3 sc, [sc in next 29{30-29-30} sc, ch 3, skip next 3 sc] 4 times, sc in last 4{6-4-6} sc.

Row 5: Ch 1, turn; (sc in each sc across to next ch-3 sp, 3 sc in ch-3 sp) 5 times, ★ sc in each sc across to next ch-1 sp, sc in ch-1 sp, place marker in sc just made; repeat from ★ once **more**, sc in each sc across.

Row 6: Ch 1, turn; ★ sc in each sc across to next marked sc, (sc, ch 1, sc) in marked sc; repeat from ★ once **more**, sc in each sc across.

Row 7: Ch 1, turn; (sc in each sc across to next ch-1 sp, sc in ch-1 sp) twice, sc in each sc across; finish off.

BOTTOM RUFFLE
Row 1: With **right** side facing, join thread with slip st in end of last row of Body Edging; ch 1, work 7 sc across end of rows on Edging, working in sps across beginning ch, work 321{353-389-429} sc evenly spaced across, work 7 sc across end of rows on Body Edging: 335{367-403-443} sc.

Row 2: Ch 1, turn; sc in first 2 sc, ch 4, skip next 3 sc, ★ sc in next sc, ch 4, skip next 3 sc; repeat from ★ across to last 2 sc, sc in last 2 sc: 83{91-100-110} ch-4 sps.

Row 3: Ch 3, turn; dc in next sc, 7 dc in each ch-4 sp across, dc in last 2 sc.

Row 4: Ch 3, turn; skip next dc, dc in each dc across to last 2 dc, skip next dc, dc in last dc.

Row 5: Ch 1, turn; sc in first dc, (ch 3, sc in next dc) across; finish off.

Sew buttons opposite buttonholes.

4. SHORT SLEEVE CARDIGAN

Size:	Small	Medium	Large	Ex-Large
Chest Measurement:	32-34"	36-38"	40-42"	44-46"
Finished Chest Measurement:	36½"	40½"	44½"	48½"

Size Note: Instructions are written for size Small with sizes Medium, Large, and Ex-Large in braces { }. Instructions will be easier to read if you circle all the numbers pertaining to your size. If only one number is given, it applies to all sizes.

MATERIALS
Bedspread Weight Cotton Thread (size 10):
   2,095{2,265-2,715-2,915} yards
Steel crochet hook, size 8 (1.50 mm) **or** size needed for gauge
Tapestry needle
⅜" Buttons - 5
Sewing needle and thread

GAUGE: 36 dc and 15 rows = 4"

Gauge Swatch: 2"w x 4"h
Ch 20.
Row 1: Dc in fourth ch from hook **(3 skipped chs count as first dc)** and in each ch across: 18 dc.
Rows 2-15: Ch 3 **(counts as first dc)**, turn; dc in next dc and in each dc across.
Finish off.

Cardigan is worked in one piece to armhole.

STITCH GUIDE

DECREASE (uses next 2 dc or ch-1 sps)
★ YO, insert hook in **next** dc or ch-1 sp indicated, YO and pull up a loop, YO and draw through 2 loops on hook; repeat from ★ once **more**, YO and draw through all 3 loops on hook.

DOUBLE DECREASE (uses next 3 dc)
★ YO, insert hook in **next** dc, YO and pull up a loop, YO and draw through 2 loops on hook; repeat from ★ 2 times **more**, YO and draw through all 4 loops on hook.

SC DECREASE
Pull up a loop in next 2 ch-1 sps, YO and draw through all 3 loops on hook.

PICOT
Ch 3, sc in third ch from hook.

Continued on page 15.

BOTTOM EDGING

Ch 327{363-399-435}, place marker in third ch from hook for st placement.

Row 1 (Right side): Dc in fourth ch from hook **(3 skipped chs count as first dc)** and in each ch across: 325{361-397-433} dc.

Note: Loop a short piece of thread around any stitch to mark Row 1 as **right** side.

Row 2: Ch 1, turn; sc in first dc, ★ ch 3, skip next 5 dc, (3 dc, ch 2, 3 dc) in next dc, ch 3, skip next 5 dc, sc in next dc; repeat from ★ across: 28{31-34-37} sc and 27{30-33-36} ch-2 sps.

Row 3: Ch 4 **(counts as first dc plus ch 1, now and throughout)**, turn; dc in next 3 dc, (2 dc, ch 2, 2 dc) in next ch-2 sp, dc in next 3 dc, ch 1, dc in next sc, ★ ch 1, dc in next 3 dc, (2 dc, ch 2, 2 dc) in next ch-2 sp, dc in next 3 dc, ch 1, dc in next sc; repeat from ★ across: 298{331-364-397} dc and 81{90-99-108} sps.

Row 4: Ch 2, turn; skip first ch-1 sp, dc in next dc, (ch 1, skip next dc, dc in next dc) twice, (ch 1, dc) 3 times in next ch-2 sp, ch 1, (dc in next dc, ch 1, skip next dc) twice, ★ double decrease, (ch 1, skip next dc, dc in next dc) twice, (ch 1, dc) 3 times in next ch-2 sp, ch 1, (dc in next dc, ch 1, skip next dc) twice; repeat from ★ across to last 2 dc, decrease in last 2 dc: 216{240-264-288} ch-1 sps.

Row 5: Ch 1, turn; sc in first st and in next ch-1 sp, work Picot, (sc in next ch-1 sp, work Picot) 6 times, ★ sc decrease, work Picot, (sc in next ch-1 sp, work Picot) 6 times; repeat from ★ across to last ch-1 sp, sc in last ch-1 sp and in last dc; finish off.

BODY

Row 1: With **right** side facing and working in free loops of beginning ch *(Fig. 2, page 1)*, join thread with slip st in first ch; ch 3 **(counts as first dc, now and throughout)**, dc in same ch and in each ch across to marked ch, 2 dc in marked ch: 327{363-399-435} dc.

Row 2: Ch 3, turn; dc in next dc and in each dc across.

Row 3: Ch 3, turn; dc in next 4 dc, ch 3, skip next 2 dc, sc in next dc, ch 3, ★ skip next 2 dc, dc in next 7 dc, ch 3, skip next 2 dc, sc in next dc, ch 3; repeat from ★ across to last 7 dc, skip next 2 dc, dc in last 5 dc: 192{213-234-255} dc and 54{60-66-72} ch-3 sps.

Row 4: Ch 3, turn; dc in next 4 dc, ch 1, sc in next ch-3 sp, ch 3, sc in next ch-3 sp, ch 1, ★ dc in next 7 dc, ch 1, sc in next ch-3 sp, ch 3, sc in next ch-3 sp, ch 1; repeat from ★ across to last 5 dc, dc in last 5 dc: 192{213-234-255} dc and 27{30-33-36} ch-3 sps.

Row 5: Ch 3, turn; dc in next 4 dc, skip next ch-1 sp, 5 dc in next ch-3 sp, ★ skip next sc and next ch-1 sp, dc in next 7 dc, skip next ch-1 sp, 5 dc in next ch-3 sp; repeat from ★ across to last sc, skip next sc and next ch-1 sp, dc in last 5 dc: 327{363-399-435} dc.

Rows 6-8: Ch 3, turn; dc in next dc and in each dc across.

Row 9: Ch 3, turn; dc in next 10 dc, ch 3, skip next 2 dc, sc in next dc, ch 3, ★ skip next 2 dc, dc in next 7 dc, ch 3, skip next 2 dc, sc in next dc, ch 3; repeat from ★ across to last 13 dc, skip next 2 dc, dc in last 11 dc: 197{218-239-260} dc and 52{58-64-70} ch-3 sps.

Row 10: Ch 3, turn; dc in next 10 dc, ch 1, sc in next ch-3 sp, ch 3, sc in next ch-3 sp, ch 1, ★ dc in next 7 dc, ch 1, sc in next ch-3 sp, ch 3, sc in next ch-3 sp, ch 1; repeat from ★ across to last 11 dc, dc in last 11 dc: 197{218-239-260} dc and 26{29-32-35} ch-3 sps.

Row 11: Ch 3, turn; dc in next 10 dc, skip next ch-1 sp, 5 dc in next ch-3 sp, ★ skip next sc and next ch-1 sp, dc in next 7 dc, skip next ch-1 sp, 5 dc in next ch-3 sp; repeat from ★ across to last sc, skip next sc and next ch-1 sp, dc in last 11 dc: 327{363-399-435} dc.

Rows 12-14: Ch 3, turn; dc in next dc and in each dc across.

Rows 15-43: Repeat Rows 3-14 twice, then repeat Rows 3-7 once **more**; do **not** finish off.

LEFT FRONT

Row 1: Ch 3, turn; dc in next 71{80-89-98} dc, leave remaining 255{282-309-336} dc unworked: 72{81-90-99} dc.

Row 2: Ch 3, turn; dc in next 7{4-1-10} dc, ch 3, skip next 2 dc, sc in next dc, ch 3, ★ skip next 2 dc, dc in next 7 dc, ch 3, skip next 2 dc, sc in next dc, ch 3; repeat from ★ across to last 13 dc, skip next 2 dc, dc in last 11 dc: 47{51-55-64} dc and 10{12-14-14} ch-3 sps.

Row 3: Ch 3, turn; dc in next 10 dc, ch 1, sc in next ch-3 sp, ch 3, sc in next ch-3 sp, ch 1, ★ dc in next 7 dc, ch 1, sc in next ch-3 sp, ch 3, sc in next ch-3 sp, ch 1; repeat from ★ across to last 8{5-2-11} dc, dc in last 8{5-2-11} dc: 47{51-55-64} dc and 5{6-7-7} ch-3 sps.

Row 4: Ch 3, turn; dc in next 7{4-1-10} dc, skip next ch-1 sp, 5 dc in next ch-3 sp, ★ skip next sc and next ch-1 sp, dc in next 7 dc, skip next ch-1 sp, 5 dc in next ch-3 sp; repeat from ★ across to last sc, skip next sc and next ch-1 sp, dc in last 11 dc: 72{81-90-99} dc.

Rows 5-7: Ch 3, turn; dc in next dc and in each dc across.

Row 8: Ch 3, turn; dc in next 1{10-7-4} dc, ch 3, skip next 2 dc, sc in next dc, ch 3, ★ skip next 2 dc, dc in next 7 dc, ch 3, skip next 2 dc, sc in next dc, ch 3; repeat from ★ across to last 7 dc, skip next 2 dc, dc in last 5 dc: 42{51-55-59} dc and 12{12-14-16} ch-3 sps.

Row 9: Ch 3, turn; dc in next 4 dc, ch 1, sc in next ch-3 sp, ch 3, sc in next ch-3 sp, ch 1, ★ dc in next 7 dc, ch 1, sc in next ch-3 sp, ch 3, sc in next ch-3 sp, ch 1; repeat from ★ across to last 2{11-8-5} dc, dc in last 2{11-8-5} dc: 42{51-55-59} dc and 6{6-7-8} ch-3 sps.

Row 10: Ch 3, turn; dc in next 1{10-7-4} dc, skip next ch-1 sp, 5 dc in next ch-3 sp, ★ skip next sc and next ch-1 sp, dc in next 7 dc, skip next ch-1 sp, 5 dc in next ch-3 sp; repeat from ★ across to last sc, skip next sc and next ch-1 sp, dc in last 5 dc: 72{81-90-99} dc.

Rows 11-13: Ch 3, turn; dc in next dc and in each dc across.

Rows 14-22: Repeat Rows 2-10; do **not** finish off: 72{81-90-99} dc.

NECK SHAPING

Row 1: Turn; slip st in first 17 dc, ch 2, dc in next dc and in each dc across: 55{64-73-82} dc.

Row 2 (Decrease row)**:** Ch 3, turn; dc in next dc and in each dc across to last 2 dc, decrease in last 2 dc: 54{63-72-81} sts.

Row 3 (Decrease row)**:** Ch 2, turn; dc in next dc and in each dc across: 53{62-71-80} dc.

Maintaining established pattern, continue to decrease one stitch at neck edge, every row, 7{9-11-13} times **more**: 46{53-60-67} sts.

Work even for 4{2-6-4} rows.

Finish off.

BACK

Row 1: With **wrong** side facing, skip next 18 dc from Left Front and join thread with slip st in next dc; ch 3, dc in next 146{164-182-200} dc, leave remaining 90{99-108-117} dc unworked: 147{165-183-201} dc.

Row 2: Ch 3, turn; dc in next 4{7-10-1} dc, ch 3, skip next 2 dc, sc in next dc, ch 3, ★ skip next 2 dc, dc in next 7 dc, ch 3, skip next 2 dc, sc in next dc, ch 3; repeat from ★ across to last 7{10-13-4} dc, skip next 2 dc, dc in last 5{8-11-2} dc: 87{100-113-116} dc and 24{26-28-34} ch-3 sps.

Row 3: Ch 3, turn; dc in next 4{7-10-1} dc, ch 1, sc in next ch-3 sp, ch 3, sc in next ch-3 sp, ch 1, ★ dc in next 7 dc, ch 1, sc in next ch-3 sp, ch 3, sc in next ch-3 sp, ch 1; repeat from ★ across to last 5{8-11-2} dc, dc in last 5{8-11-2} dc: 87{100-113-116} dc and 12{13-14-17} ch-3 sps.

Row 4: Ch 3, turn; dc in next 4{7-10-1} dc, skip next ch-1 sp, 5 dc in next ch-3 sp, ★ skip next sc and next ch-1 sp, dc in next 7 dc, skip next ch-1 sp, 5 dc in next ch-3 sp; repeat from ★ across to last sc, skip next sc and next ch-1 sp, dc in last 5{8-11-2} dc: 147{165-183-201} dc.

Rows 5-7: Ch 3, turn; dc in next dc and in each dc across.

Row 8: Ch 3, turn; dc in next 10{1-4-7} dc, ch 3, skip next 2 dc, sc in next dc, ch 3, ★ skip next 2 dc, dc in next 7 dc, ch 3, skip next 2 dc, sc in next dc, ch 3; repeat from ★ across to last 13{4-7-10} dc, skip next 2 dc, dc in last 11{2-5-8} dc: 92{95-108-121} dc and 22{28-30-32} ch-3 sps.

Row 9: Ch 3, turn; dc in next 10{1-4-7} dc, ch 1, sc in next ch-3 sp, ch 3, sc in next ch-3 sp, ch 1, ★ dc in next 7 dc, ch 1, sc in next ch-3 sp, ch 3, sc in next ch-3 sp, ch 1; repeat from ★ across to last 11{2-5-8} dc, dc in last 11{2-5-8} dc: 92{95-108-121} dc and 11{14-15-16} ch-3 sps.

Row 10: Ch 3, turn; dc in next 10{1-4-7} dc, skip next ch-1 sp, 5 dc in next ch-3 sp, ★ skip next sc and next ch-1 sp, dc in next 7 dc, skip next ch-1 sp, 5 dc in next ch-3 sp; repeat from ★ across to last sc, skip next sc and next ch-1 sp, dc in last 11{2-5-8} dc: 147{165-183-201} dc.

Rows 11-13: Ch 3, turn; dc in next dc and in each dc across.

Rows 14 thru 36{36-42-42}: Repeat Rows 2-13, 1{1-2-2} time(s); then repeat Rows 2 thru 12{12-6-6} once **more**.

Finish off.

RIGHT FRONT

Row 1: With **wrong** side facing, skip next 18 dc from Back and join thread with slip st in next dc; ch 3, dc in next dc and in each dc across: 72{81-90-99} dc.

Row 2: Ch 3, turn; dc in next 10 dc, ch 3, skip next 2 dc, sc in next dc, ch 3, ★ skip next 2 dc, dc in next 7 dc, ch 3, skip next 2 dc, sc in next dc, ch 3; repeat from ★ across to last 10{7-4-13} dc, skip next 2 dc, dc in last 8{5-2-11} dc: 47{51-55-64} dc and 10{12-14-14} ch-3 sps.

Row 3: Ch 3, turn; dc in next 7{4-1-10} dc, ch 1, sc in next ch-3 sp, ch 3, sc in next ch-3 sp, ch 1, ★ dc in next 7 dc, ch 1, sc in next ch-3 sp, ch 3, sc in next ch-3 sp, ch 1; repeat from ★ across to last 11 dc, dc in last 11 dc: 47{51-55-64} dc and 5{6-7-7} ch-3 sps.

Row 4: Ch 3, turn; dc in next 10 dc, skip next ch-1 sp, 5 dc in next ch-3 sp, ★ skip next sc and next ch-1 sp, dc in next 7 dc, skip next ch-1 sp, 5 dc in next ch-3 sp; repeat from ★ across to last sc, skip next sc and next ch-1 sp, dc in last 8{5-2-11} dc: 72{81-90-99} dc.

Rows 5-7: Ch 3, turn; dc in next dc and in each dc across.

Row 8: Ch 3, turn; dc in next 4 dc, ch 3, skip next 2 dc, sc in next dc, ch 3, ★ skip next 2 dc, dc in next 7 dc, ch 3, skip next 2 dc, sc in next dc, ch 3; repeat from ★ across to last 4{13-10-7} dc, skip next 2 dc, dc in last 2{11-8-5} dc: 42{51-55-59} dc and 12{12-14-16} ch-3 sps.

Row 9: Ch 3, turn; dc in next 1{10-7-4} dc, ch 1, sc in next ch-3 sp, ch 3, sc in next ch-3 sp, ch 1, ★ dc in next 7 dc, ch 1, sc in next ch-3 sp, ch 3, sc in next ch-3 sp, ch 1; repeat from ★ across to last 5 dc, dc in last 5 dc: 42{51-55-59} dc and 6{6-7-8} ch-3 sps.

Row 10: Ch 3, turn; dc in next 4 dc, skip next ch-1 sp, 5 dc in next ch-3 sp, ★ skip next sc and next ch-1 sp, dc in next 7 dc, skip next ch-1 sp, 5 dc in next ch-3 sp; repeat from ★ across to last sc, skip next sc and next ch-1 sp, dc in last 2{11-8-5} dc: 72{81-90-99} dc.

Rows 11-13: Ch 3, turn; dc in next dc and in each dc across.

Rows 14-22: Repeat Rows 2-10; do **not** finish off: 72{81-90-99} dc.

Continued on page 17.

NECK SHAPING

Row 1: Ch 3, turn; dc in next 53{62-71-80} dc, decrease in next 2 dc, leave remaining 16 dc unworked: 55{64-73-82} sts.

Row 2: Ch 2, turn; dc in next dc and in each dc across: 54{63-72-81} dc.

Row 3: Ch 3, turn; dc in next dc and in each dc across to last 2 dc, decrease in last 2 dc: 53{62-71-80} sts.

Maintaining established pattern, continue to decrease one stitch at neck edge, every row, 7{9-11-13} times **more**: 46{53-60-67} dc.

Work even for 4{2-6-4} rows.

Finish off.

SLEEVE (Make 2)

Ch 171{171-207-207}.

Work same as Bottom Edging, page 15.

Work same as Body, page 15, for 19 rows; do **not** finish off: 171{171-207-207} dc.

CAP

Row 1: Turn; slip st in first 24{24-30-30} dc, sc in next 24{24-30-30} dc, hdc in next 24{24-30-30} dc, dc in next 27 dc, hdc in next 24{24-30-30} dc, sc in next 24{24-30-30} dc, leave remaining 24{24-30-30} dc unworked: 123{123-147-147} sts.

Row 2: Turn; slip st in first 18{18-22-22} sc, sc in next 17{17-21-21} sts, hdc in next 17{17-21-21} sts, dc in next 19 dc, hdc in next 17{17-21-21} sts, sc in next 17{17-21-21} sts, leave remaining 18{18-22-22} sc unworked; finish off.

FINISHING

Sew shoulder seams.

Sew last row on Sleeve to end of rows along armhole edge, matching center of Sleeve to shoulder seam; sew unworked sts of armhole to end of rows on Sleeve.

Weave Sleeve seam *(Fig. 3, page 1)*.

BODY EDGING

Row 1: With **right** side facing and working in end of rows across Right Front, join thread with slip st in last row on Bottom Edging; ch 1, work 158 sc evenly spaced across, working across unworked dc, sc in next dc, place marker in sc just made, sc in next 15 dc, work 36{36-50-50} sc evenly spaced along neck edge, work 55{59-63-67} sc across Back, work 36{36-50-50} sc evenly spaced along neck edge, sc in next 16 dc, place marker in last sc made, work 158 sc evenly spaced across Left Front: 475{479-511-515} sc.

Row 2: Ch 1, turn; ★ sc in each sc across to next marked sc, (sc, ch 1, sc) in marked sc; repeat from ★ once **more**, sc in each sc across: 477{481-513-517} sc.

Row 3 (Buttonhole row): Ch 1, turn; sc in first 5 sc, ch 3, ★ skip next 3 sc, sc in next 34 sc, ch 3; repeat from ★ 3 times **more**, skip next 3 sc, (sc in each sc across to next ch-1 sp, sc in ch-1 sp, place marker in sc just made) twice, sc in each sc across.

Row 4: Ch 1, turn; ★ sc in each sc across to next marked sc, (sc, ch 1, sc) in marked sc; repeat from ★ once **more**, (sc in each sc across to next ch-3 sp, 3 sc in ch-3 sp) 5 times, sc in each sc across: 481{485-517-521} sc.

Row 5: Ch 1, turn; ★ sc in each sc across to next ch-1 sp, sc in ch-1 sp, place marker in sc just made; repeat from ★ once **more**, sc in each sc across; finish off.

COLLAR

Row 1: With **wrong** side facing and working in Back Loops Only of Row 5 *(Fig. 1, page 1)*, join thread with slip st in first sc to left of marker on Left Front Body Edging; ch 3, dc in next 14 sc, 2 dc in next sc, (dc in next sc, 2 dc in next sc) 6 times, [dc in next 4{1-7-3} sc, 2 dc in next sc] 4{8-4-8} times, (dc in next sc, 2 dc in next sc) 5 times, dc in next 45{57-57-61} sc, 2 dc in next sc, (dc in next sc, 2 dc in next sc) 5 times, [dc in next 4{1-7-3} sc, 2 dc in next sc] 4{8-4-8} times, (dc in next sc, 2 dc in next sc) 6 times, dc in next 15 sc, leave remaining sc unworked: 193{205-229-241} dc.

Row 2: Ch 1, turn; sc in first dc, ★ ch 5, skip next 5 dc, (dc, ch 3, dc) in next dc, ch 5, skip next 5 dc, sc in next dc; repeat from ★ across: 17{18-20-21} sc and 48{51-57-60} sps.

Row 3: Ch 1, turn; sc in first sc, ★ ch 4, skip next ch-5 sp, (2 dc, ch 2, 2 dc) in next ch-3 sp, ch 4, skip next ch-5 sp, sc in next sc; repeat from ★ across.

Row 4: Ch 1, turn; sc in first sc, ★ ch 3, (3 dc, ch 2, 3 dc) in next ch-2 sp, ch 3, sc in next sc; repeat from ★ across.

Row 5: Ch 4, turn; dc in next 3 dc, (2 dc, ch 2, 2 dc) in next ch-2 sp, dc in next 3 dc, ch 1, dc in next sc, ★ ch 1, dc in next 3 dc, (2 dc, ch 2, 2 dc) in next ch-2 sp, dc in next 3 dc, ch 1, dc in next sc; repeat from ★ across.

Row 6: Ch 3, turn; dc in next dc, (ch 1, skip next dc, dc in next dc) twice, ch 1, (dc, ch 1) 3 times in next ch-2 sp, dc in next dc, (ch 1, skip next dc, dc in next dc) twice, ★ ch 1, decrease in next 2 ch-1 sps, ch 1, dc in next dc, (ch 1, skip next dc, dc in next dc) twice, ch 1, (dc, ch 1) 3 times in next ch-2 sp, dc in next dc, (ch 1, skip next dc, dc in next dc) twice; repeat from ★ across to last dc, dc in last dc.

Row 7: Ch 1, turn; sc in first dc and in next ch-1 sp, (work Picot, sc in next ch-1 sp) 7 times, ★ work Picot, sc decrease, (work Picot, sc in next ch-1 sp) 8 times; repeat from ★ across to last 2 dc, skip next dc, sc in last dc; finish off.

Sew buttons opposite buttonholes.

5. CREWNECK PULLOVER

Size:	Small	Medium	Large	Ex-Large
Chest Measurement:	32-34"	36-38"	40-42"	44-46"
Finished Chest Measurement:	37"	40"	45"	48"

Size Note: Instructions are written for size Small with sizes Medium, Large, and Ex-Large in braces { }. Instructions will be easier to read if you circle all the numbers pertaining to your size. If only one number is given, it applies to all sizes.

MATERIALS

J. & P. Coats Luster Sheen®:
  18{20-23-25} ounces,
    [510{570-650-710} grams,
      1,545{1,715-1,970-2,145} yards]
Crochet hook, size D (3.25 mm) **or** size needed
  for gauge
Tapestry needle
Safety pin

GAUGE: In Body pattern, (dc, ch 1, dc) 9 times
  and 12 rows = 4"

Gauge Swatch: 4"w x 2"h
Work same as Bottom Border through Row 6.

Pullover is worked in one piece to armhole.

STITCH GUIDE

PICOT
Ch 3, sc in third ch from hook.

SC DECREASE
Pull up a loop in next 2 ch-1 sps, YO and draw through all 3 loops on hook.

DC DECREASE (uses next 2 sts)
★ YO, insert hook in **next** st, YO and pull up a loop, YO and draw through 2 loops on hook; repeat from ★ once **more**, YO and draw through all 3 loops on hook.

REVERSE SINGLE CROCHET
(abbreviated reverse sc)
Working from **left** to **right**, insert hook in st indicated to right of hook *(Fig. 4a)*, YO and draw through, under and to left of loop on hook (2 loops on hook) *(Fig. 4b)*, YO and draw through both loops on hook *(Fig. 4c)* (reverse sc made, *Fig. 4d*).

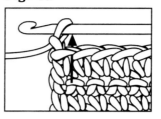

Fig. 4a

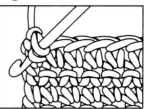

Fig. 4b

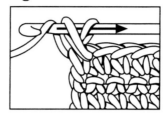

Fig. 4c

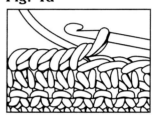

Fig. 4d

BOTTOM BORDER
Leaving a long end for sewing, ch 31 **loosely**.

Row 1 (Right side): (Dc, ch 1) twice in sixth ch from hook, skip next ch, sc in next ch, ch 1, skip next ch, dc in next 8 chs, ch 5, skip next 2 chs, dc in next 8 chs, ch 1, skip next ch, sc in next ch, ch 1, skip next ch, (dc, ch 1, dc) in last ch: 20 dc and 8 sps.

Note: Loop a short piece of yarn around any stitch to mark Row 1 as **right** side.

Row 2: Ch 5, turn; (dc, ch 1, dc) in first ch-1 sp, ch 3, skip next 2 ch-1 sps, dc in next 4 dc, ch 5, sc in next ch-5 sp, ch 5, skip next 4 dc, dc in next 4 dc, ch 3, skip next 2 ch-1 sps, (dc, ch 1, dc) in next ch-1 sp, leave remaining sts unworked: 12 dc and 7 sps.

Row 3: Ch 5, turn; (dc, ch 1) twice in first ch-1 sp, sc in next ch-3 sp, ch 1, dc in next 2 dc, ch 5, (sc in next ch-5 sp, ch 5) twice, skip next 2 dc, dc in next 2 dc, ch 1, sc in next ch-3 sp, (ch 1, dc) twice in next ch-1 sp, leave remaining sts unworked: 8 dc and 10 sps.

Row 4: Ch 5, turn; (dc, ch 1, dc) in first ch-1 sp, ch 3, skip next 2 ch-1 sps, dc in next 2 dc, 2 dc in next ch-5 sp, ch 5, sc in next ch-5 sp, ch 5, 2 dc in next ch-5 sp, dc in next 2 dc, ch 3, skip next 2 ch-1 sps, (dc, ch 1, dc) in next ch-1 sp, leave remaining sts unworked: 12 dc and 7 sps.

Row 5: Ch 5, turn; (dc, ch 1) twice in first ch-1 sp, sc in next ch-3 sp, ch 1, dc in next 4 dc, 4 dc in next ch-5 sp, ch 5, 4 dc in next ch-5 sp, dc in next 4 dc, ch 1, sc in next ch-3 sp, (ch 1, dc) twice in next ch-1 sp, leave remaining sts unworked: 20 dc and 8 sps.

Continued on page 19.

Rows 6 thru 112{120-136-144}: Repeat Rows 2-5, 26{28-32-34} times; then repeat Rows 2-4 once **more**; do **not** finish off: 12 dc and 7 sps.

Slip loop onto safety pin to keep piece from unraveling while sewing seam. With **right** side together and using long end, sew first and last rows together working in sts across last row and in free loops of beginning ch *(Fig. 2, page 1)*.

TRIM

Rnd 1: With **right** side facing, remove safety pin and slip loop onto hook, slip st in first 2 chs on Row 1 and in same sp, ch 3, (dc, ch 2, 2 dc) in same sp, working in end of rows, (2 dc, ch 2, 2 dc) in each ch-5 sp around; join with slip st to top of beginning ch-3: 56{60-68-72} ch-2 sps.

Rnd 2: Do **not** turn; slip st in next dc and in next ch-2 sp, ch 1, sc in same sp, (ch 1, dc) 5 times in next ch-2 sp, ★ ch 1, sc in next ch-2 sp, (ch 1, dc) 5 times in next ch-2 sp; repeat from ★ around, sc in first sc to form last ch-1 sp.

Rnd 3: Ch 1, pull up a loop in same sp and in next ch-1 sp, YO and draw through all 3 loops on hook, work Picot, (sc in next ch-1 sp, work Picot) 4 times, ★ sc decrease, work Picot, (sc in next ch-1 sp, work Picot) 4 times; repeat from ★ around; join with slip st to first st, finish off.

BODY

Rnd 1: With **right** side facing and working in ch-5 sps across end of rows, join yarn with slip st in first ch-5 sp to left of seam; ch 4 **(counts as first dc plus ch 1, now and throughout)**, (2 dc, ch 1, dc) in same sp, (dc, ch 1, dc) in next ch-5 sp, ★ (dc, ch 1, 2 dc, ch 1, dc) in next ch-5 sp, (dc, ch 1, dc) in next ch-5 sp; repeat from ★ around; join with slip st to first dc: 84{90-102-108} ch-1 sps.

Rnd 2: Turn; slip st in next dc and in next ch-1 sp, ch 4, dc in same sp, (dc, ch 1, dc) in next ch-1 sp and in each ch-1 sp around; join with slip st to first dc.

Repeat Rnd 2 until piece measures approximately 14{14½-15-15½}" from Rnd 3 of Trim, ending by working a **wrong** side rnd; do **not** finish off.

BACK

Row 1: Turn; slip st in next 7 sts and in next ch-1 sp, ch 3 **(counts as first dc, now and throughout)**, (dc, ch 1, dc) in next 36{39-45-48} ch-1 sps, dc in next ch-1 sp, leave remaining ch-1 sps unworked: 36{39-45-48} ch-1 sps.

Row 2: Ch 3, turn; (dc, ch 1, dc) in each ch-1 sp across, skip next dc, dc in last dc.

Repeat Row 2 until Back measures approximately 9{9½-10-10½}", ending by working a **right** side row; finish off.

FRONT

Row 1: With **right** side facing, skip next 4 ch-1 sps from Back and join yarn with slip st in next ch-1 sp; ch 3, (dc, ch 1, dc) in next 36{39-45-48} ch-1 sps, dc in next ch-1 sp, leave remaining ch-1 sps unworked: 36{39-45-48} ch-1 sps.

Row 2: Ch 3, turn; (dc, ch 1, dc) in each ch-1 sp across, skip next dc, dc in last dc.

Repeat Row 2 until Front measures approximately 5{5½-6-6½}", ending by working a **wrong** side row; do **not** finish off.

LEFT NECK SHAPING

Row 1: Ch 3, turn; (dc, ch 1, dc) in next 13{14-17-18} ch-1 sps, dc in next ch-1 sp, leave remaining 22{24-27-29} ch-1 sps unworked: 13{14-17-18} ch-1 sps.

Row 2 (Decrease row): Ch 3, turn; dc in next ch-1 sp, (dc, ch 1, dc) in next ch-1 sp and in each ch-1 sp across, skip next dc, dc in last dc: 12{13-16-17} ch-1 sps.

Row 3: Ch 3, turn; (dc, ch 1, dc) in each ch-1 sp across, skip next dc, dc in last 2 dc.

Row 4: Ch 2, turn; dc in next dc, (dc, ch 1, dc) in each ch-1 sp across to last 2 dc, skip next dc, dc in last dc.

Row 5: Ch 3, turn; (dc, ch 1, dc) in each ch-1 sp across, skip next dc, dc in last dc.

Rows 6-13: Repeat Rows 2-5 twice: 10{11-14-15} ch-1 sps.

Finish off.

RIGHT NECK SHAPING

Row 1: With **right** side facing, skip next 8{9-9-10} ch-1 sps from Left Neck Shaping and join yarn with slip st in next ch-1 sp; ch 3, (dc, ch 1, dc) in next ch-1 sp and in each ch-1 sp across, skip next dc, dc in last dc: 13{14-17-18} ch-1 sps.

Row 2 (Decrease row): Ch 3, turn; (dc, ch 1, dc) in each ch-1 sp across to last ch-1 sp, dc in last ch-1 sp, skip next dc, dc in last dc: 12{13-16-17} ch-1 sps.

Row 3: Ch 3, turn; dc in next dc, (dc, ch 1, dc) in each ch-1 sp across, skip next dc, dc in last dc.

Row 4: Ch 3, turn; (dc, ch 1, dc) in each ch-1 sp across, skip next dc, dc decrease.

Row 5: Ch 3, turn; (dc, ch 1, dc) in each ch-1 sp across, skip next dc, dc in last dc.

Rows 6-13: Repeat Rows 2-5 twice: 10{11-14-15} ch-1 sps.

Finish off.

SLEEVE (Make 2)
BOTTOM BORDER
Leaving a long end for sewing, ch 31 **loosely**.

Row 1 (Right side)**:** (Dc, ch 1) twice in sixth ch from hook, skip next ch, sc in next ch, ch 1, skip next ch, dc in next 8 chs, ch 5, skip next 2 chs, dc in next 8 chs, ch 1, skip next ch, sc in next ch, ch 1, skip next ch, (dc, ch 1, dc) in last ch: 20 dc and 8 sps.

Note: Mark Row 1 as **right** side.

Row 2: Ch 5, turn; (dc, ch 1, dc) in first ch-1 sp, ch 3, skip next 2 ch-1 sps, dc in next 4 dc, ch 5, sc in next ch-5 sp, ch 5, skip next 4 dc, dc in next 4 dc, ch 3, skip next 2 ch-1 sps, (dc, ch 1, dc) in next ch-1 sp, leave remaining sts unworked: 12 dc and 7 sps.

Row 3: Ch 5, turn; (dc, ch 1) twice in first ch-1 sp, sc in next ch-3 sp, ch 1, dc in next 2 dc, ch 5, (sc in next ch-5 sp, ch 5) twice, skip next 2 dc, dc in next 2 dc, ch 1, sc in next ch-3 sp, (ch 1, dc) twice in next ch-1 sp, leave remaining sts unworked: 8 dc and 10 sps.

Row 4: Ch 5, turn; (dc, ch 1, dc) in first ch-1 sp, ch 3, skip next 2 ch-1 sps, dc in next 2 dc, 2 dc in next ch-5 sp, ch 5, sc in next ch-5 sp, ch 5, 2 dc in next ch-5 sp, dc in next 2 dc, ch 3, skip next 2 ch-1 sps, (dc, ch 1, dc) in next ch-1 sp, leave remaining sts unworked: 12 dc and 7 sps.

Row 5: Ch 5, turn; (dc, ch 1) twice in first ch-1 sp, sc in next ch-3 sp, ch 1, dc in next 4 dc, 4 dc in next ch-5 sp, ch 5, 4 dc in next ch-5 sp, dc in next 4 dc, ch 1, sc in next ch-3 sp, (ch 1, dc) twice in next ch-1 sp, leave remaining sts unworked: 20 dc and 8 sps.

Rows 6 thru 24{28-28-28}: Repeat Rows 2-5, 4{5-5-5} times; then repeat Rows 2-4 once **more**; do **not** finish off: 12 dc and 7 sps.

Slip loop onto safety pin to keep piece from unraveling while sewing seam. With **right** side together and using long end, sew first and last rows together working in sts across last row and in free loops of beginning ch.

TRIM
Rnd 1: With **right** side facing, remove safety pin and slip loop onto hook, slip st in first 2 chs on Row 1 and in same sp, ch 3, (dc, ch 2, 2 dc) in same sp, working in end of rows, (2 dc, ch 2, 2 dc) in each ch-5 sp around; join with slip st to first dc: 12{14-14-14} ch-2 sps.

Rnd 2: Do **not** turn; slip st in next dc and in next ch-2 sp, ch 1, sc in same sp, (ch 1, dc) 5 times in next ch-2 sp, ★ ch 1, sc in next ch-2 sp, (ch 1, dc) 5 times in next ch-2 sp; repeat from ★ around, sc in first sc to form last ch-1 sp.

Rnd 3: Ch 1, pull up a loop in same sp and in next ch-1 sp, YO and draw through all 3 loops on hook, work Picot, (sc in next ch-1 sp, work Picot) 4 times, ★ sc decrease, work Picot, (sc in next ch-1 sp, work Picot) 4 times; repeat from ★ around; join with slip st to first st, finish off.

BODY
Row 1: With **right** side facing and working in ch-5 sps across end of rows, join yarn with slip st in first ch-5 sp to left of seam; ch 4, (dc, ch 1, dc) in same sp, [dc, (ch 1, dc) twice] in next 5 ch-5 sps, (dc, ch 1, dc) in next 1{3-3-3} ch-5 sp(s), [dc, (ch 1, dc) twice] in last 5 ch-5 sps; do **not** join: 23{25-25-25} ch-1 sps.

Row 2: Ch 3, turn; (dc, ch 1, dc) in each ch-1 sp across, dc in last dc.

Row 3: Ch 3, turn; (dc, ch 1, dc) in each ch-1 sp across, skip next dc, dc in last dc.

Row 4 (Increase row)**:** Ch 4, turn; dc in same st, (dc, ch 1, dc) in each ch-1 sp across, skip next dc, (dc, ch 1, dc) in last dc: 25{27-27-27} ch-1 sps.

Row 5: Ch 3, turn; (dc, ch 1, dc) in each ch-1 sp across, dc in last dc.

Rows 6 and 7: Ch 3, turn; (dc, ch 1, dc) in each ch-1 sp across, skip next dc, dc in last dc.

Rows 8 thru 37{37-41-45}: Repeat Rows 4-7, 7{7-8-9} times; then repeat Rows 4 and 5 once **more**: 41{43-45-47} ch-1 sps.

Repeat Row 6, 2{4-2-0} times *(see Zeros, page 1)*.

Finish off.

FINISHING
Sew shoulder seams.

Sew last row on Sleeve to end of rows along armhole edge, matching center of Sleeve to shoulder seam; sew unworked sts of armhole to end of rows on Sleeve.

Weave Sleeve seams *(Fig. 3, page 1)*.

NECK EDGING
Rnd 1: With **right** side facing, join yarn with slip st in right shoulder seam; ch 1, work an even number of sc evenly spaced around neck opening; join with slip st to first sc.

Rnd 2: Ch 1, do **not** turn; working from **left** to **right**, ★ work reverse sc in next sc *(Figs. 4a-d, page 18)*, ch 1, skip next sc; repeat from ★ around; join with slip st to first st, finish off.

6. MOTIF CARDIGAN

Size: Chest Measurement:	Small	Medium	Large
	30-34"	36-40"	42-46"
Finished Chest Measurement:	36"	42"	48"

Size Note: Instructions are written for size Small with sizes Medium and Large in braces { }. Instructions will be easier to read if you circle all the numbers pertaining to your size. If only one number is given, it applies to all sizes.

MATERIALS
J. & P. Coats Luster Sheen®:
24{27-29} ounces, [680{770-820} grams, 2,055{2,315-2,485} yards]
Crochet hook, size E (3.50 mm) **or** size needed for gauge
3/8" Buttons - 5
Sewing needle and thread

GAUGE: One Motif slightly stretched = 3"

Gauge Swatch: 1¾" diameter
Work same as Motif through Rnd 2.

STITCH GUIDE

BEGINNING CLUSTER
Ch 2, ★ YO, insert hook in sp indicated, YO and pull up a loop, YO and draw through 2 loops on hook; repeat from ★ once **more**, YO and draw through all 3 loops on hook.

CLUSTER (uses one sp)
★ YO, insert hook in sp indicated, YO and pull up a loop, YO and draw through 2 loops on hook; repeat from ★ 2 times **more**, YO and draw through all 4 loops on hook.

SCALLOP
Slip st in st indicated, ch 3, 2 dc in same st.

MOTIF [Make 134{154-164}]
Ch 6; join with slip st to form a ring.

Rnd 1 (Right side)**:** Ch 6, (dc in ring, ch 3) 7 times; join with slip st to third ch of beginning ch-6: 8 ch-3 sps.

Note: Loop a short piece of yarn around any stitch to mark Rnd 1 as **right** side.

Rnd 2: Slip st in first ch-3 sp, (ch 1, sc, ch 2, 3 dc, ch 2, sc) in same sp and in each ch-3 sp around, sc in first sc to form last ch-1 sp: 8 petals.

Rnd 3: Ch 1, sc in same sp, ch 5, (sc in next ch-1 sp between petals, ch 5) around; join with slip st to first sc: 8 ch-5 sps.

Rnd 4: Slip st in first ch-5 sp, work (Beginning Cluster, ch 3, Cluster) in same sp, ch 5, sc in next ch-5 sp, ch 5, ★ work (Cluster, ch 3, Cluster) in next ch-5 sp, ch 5, sc in next ch-5 sp, ch 5; repeat from ★ 2 times **more**; join with slip st to top of Beginning Cluster.

Rnds 5 and 6: Slip st in first ch-3 sp, work (Beginning Cluster, ch 3, Cluster) in same sp, ch 5, ★ (sc in next ch-5 sp, ch 5) across to next ch-3 sp, work (Cluster, ch 3, Cluster) in ch-3 sp, ch 5; repeat from ★ 2 times **more**, (sc in next ch-5 sp, ch 5) across; join with slip st to top of Beginning Cluster.

Finish off.

HALF MOTIF [Make 6{2-6}]
Ch 4; join with slip st to form a ring.

Row 1: Ch 6, dc in ring, (ch 3, dc in ring) 4 times: 5 sps.

Row 2 (Right side)**:** Turn; slip st in first ch-3 sp, (ch 1, sc, ch 2, 3 dc, ch 2, sc) in same sp and in each sp across: 5 petals.

Note: Mark Row 2 as **right** side.

Row 3: Ch 1, turn; sc in first sc, ch 5, (sc in next ch-1 sp between petals, ch 5) across, sc in last sc: 5 ch-5 sps.

Row 4: Turn; slip st in first ch-5 sp, work (Beginning Cluster, ch 3, Cluster) in same sp, ★ ch 5, sc in next ch-5 sp, ch 5, work (Cluster, ch 3, Cluster) in next ch-5 sp; repeat from ★ once **more**.

Rows 5 and 6: Turn; slip st in first ch-3 sp, work (Beginning Cluster, ch 3, Cluster) in same sp, ★ ch 5, (sc in next ch-5 sp, ch 5) across to next ch-3 sp, work (Cluster, ch 3, Cluster) in ch-3 sp; repeat from ★ once **more**.

Finish off.

ASSEMBLY
Using Placement Diagram as a guide, page 22, join Motifs and Half Motifs together forming strips, then join strips, leaving edges of Motifs along dotted lines unjoined.

Join Motifs as follows:
With **right** sides together and working through **both** pieces, join yarn with slip st in corner ch-3 sp; ch 1, sc in same sp, ch 4, (sc in next ch-5 sp, ch 4) across to next corner ch-3 sp, sc in corner ch-3 sp; finish off.

Join strips as follows:
With **right** sides together and working through **both** pieces, join yarn with slip st in first corner ch-3 sp; ch 1, sc in same sp, ch 4, (sc in next ch-5 sp, ch 4) 4 times, sc in next corner ch-3 sp, ★ ch 1, sc in corner ch-3 sp of next Motif, ch 4, (sc in next ch-5 sp, ch 4) 4 times, sc in next corner ch-3 sp; repeat from ★ across; finish off.

SIZES SMALL AND LARGE ONLY
Join sleeve and side seams in same manner as joining strips.